Easy Step by Step guide

To

Successful Selling

By

Pauline Rowson

Rowmark

Published by   Rowmark Limited
               65 Rogers Mead
               Hayling Island
               Hampshire
               PO11 0PL

ISBN 0-9532987-4-4

Copyright Pauline Rowson 2000

The right of Pauline Rowson to be identified as the author of this work has been asserted by her in accordance with the Copyright, Design and Patents Act 1988.

Other than as permitted under the Copyright Act 1956, no part of this publication may be photocopied, recorded or otherwise reproduced, stored in a retrieval system or transmitted in any form by electronic or mechanical means without the prior permission of the copyright owner.

Printed in Great Britain by RPM Reprographics Ltd. Chichester.
Set in Arial 11

Note: The material contained in this book is set out in good faith for general guidance and no liability can be accepted for loss or expense incurred as a result of relying in particular circumstances on statements made in this book.

All rights reserved. No part of this publication may be reproduced in any material form (including photocopying or storing it in any medium by electronic means and whether or not transiently or incidentally to some other use of publication) without the written permission of the copyright owner except in accordance with the provisions of the Copyright, Designs and Patents Act 1988 or under the terms of a licence issued by the Copyright Licensing Agency Ltd. 90 Tottenham Court Road, London, England W1P 9HE. Applications for the copyright owner's written permission to reproduce any part of this publication should be addressed to the publisher.

Warning: The doing of an unauthorised act in relation to a copyright work may result in both a civil claim for damages and criminal prosecution.

About the author

Pauline Rowson is Managing Director of Rowmark Limited, a Marketing, Media, Training and Publishing organisation. She is qualified in marketing and is a member of the Chartered Institute of Marketing. She advises many businesses on all aspects of their marketing, publicity and sales. In addition, she runs training courses in marketing, sales, management and personal development.

In her spare time she is a writer of fiction.

CONTENTS

Introduction 7

How to use this guide 7

Chapter One
Why is selling important 8
What you will learn from this guide 9
Who makes a good salesperson 9
The difference between marketing & selling 10
Selling to the right person 12
The Decision Making Unit 12
In summary 17

Chapter Two
Understanding buyer behaviour 20
What influences someone? 20
Selling a service 23
In summary 25

Chapter Three
Understanding buying motivations 27
Negative buying motivations 28
Positive buying motivations 29
Switching from negative to positive 30
In summary 34

Chapter Four
Know your product/service 35
Features and benefits 35
In summary 40

Chapter Five
Know your market place and competitors 42

Getting ready for the sales interview	43
Pre-sales research	43
Set your objectives	44
Presentation material	45
In summary	46

Chapter Six

The sales interview	48
Approach	48
Your appearance	51
Your body language	54
Setting the tone	55
At an exhibition	56
In summary	57

Chapter Seven

The sales interview	60
Discussion	60
Open questions	61
Closed questions	62
Open Situation Questions	63
Diagnose	69
Comparative questions	69
Interpretation and needs	71
Listening actively	73
The sales interview summarised	75
In summary	77

Chapter Eight

Handling objections	79
Some golden rules	82
In summary	87

Chapter Nine

Closing	88
Solving the prospect's problem	89

Alternative close	90
Fear close	91
Assumptive close	92
Buying signals close	93
In summary	94

Chapter Ten

Body language	95
Personal distance	96
Body movements	96
Facial expressions and eye contact	98
Body posture	99
Impressive signals	100
In summary	101

Chapter Eleven

Selling to different personalities	104
Dominant individuals	105
Social individuals	107
Measured individuals	109
Compliant individuals	111
Selling to the opposite gender	113
In summary	115

Checklists 117

Other guides in the series 120

Introduction

The function of selling, in Britain at least, has often been considered a rather nasty occupation. This, I believe, is cultural and goes back to the days of when being in 'trade' wasn't quite the done thing! Other cultures don't have half as much of a problem with selling as the British do. To many it is a way of life and bartering is an art form. The British may be getting better at bartering and at searching out and expecting the best deal but we still don't like being sold to and we don't like people selling to us. Yet how can we succeed unless we sell our products and services?

Whether we like it or not we are all in the business of selling. People buy people which means we all need to sell ourselves. But how do we do this? This book will show you. It will also provide you with a structure to help you drive the sales process to a successful outcome. I hope you enjoy reading it.

How to use this guide

This guide is written in as clear a style as possible to help you. I recommend that you read it through from beginning to end and then dip into it to refresh your memory. The boxes in each chapter contain tips to help you and at the end of each chapter is a handy summary of the points covered.

Chapter one

Why is selling important to us?

Quite simply selling is important because unless someone sells something there is no business. We are all in the business of selling: selling ourselves, our company and our products or services. We are all sales people from the person on the reception desk to those in administration, from the van driver to the sales representative out on the road.

When we answer the telephone, when we drive our vans with the company name on it, when we visit someone, when we attend a training course or meet someone at a function, when we talk to existing customers and when we target prospects **we are selling.**

So how can we ensure we are more effective in the art of selling?

We have to get people to like us. We have to find out what their needs are. We also have to identify their company needs and problems. Then we have to provide solutions that will fulfill those needs and solve those problems. This is what we are going to look at in this book.

I will also give you a sales structure that, hopefully, will work for you. It does for me. It is called **A.D.D.I.N.** Quite simply by following the structure correctly and taking on board the other points mentioned in this book I hope you will **add in** your product or service to your prospect's organisation or life and so make a sale.

What you will learn from this guide

This guide will show you:

- how to build a greater rapport with your prospects, get them to like you and therefore increase your chances of selling to them

- how to use a sales structure that works

- how to use the buying motivations to get people to buy

- how to handle objections and close the sale.

So who makes a good salesperson?

With the right training and an awareness and understanding of others most people can become good sales people. A good salesperson is:

- someone who prepares well, who does his/her research before the visit

- someone who knows the market place and the competition

- someone who knows his or her products or

services

- someone who is a good listener, who does not always have a desire to talk about himself or herself

- someone who likes people and understands them and can develop an empathy with them.

What is the difference between selling and marketing?

Many people get confused between the terms selling and marketing. They often think they mean the same but they don't. Firstly then let us define what is meant by marketing and where selling fits into the equation.

Marketing is a complete business philosophy.

Marketing means putting the customer at the centre of your business. It involves you knowing your customers and communicating with them in the most effective way in order to win more business from them.

It is about understanding who your customers are and anticipating what they want, not just today or tomorrow, but next year, the year after, and so on.

The definition from the **Chartered Institute of Marketing** sums this up very well.

> '**Marketing is the management process responsible for identifying, anticipating and satisfying customer requirements profitably.**'
>
> **Chartered Institute of Marketing**

So where does selling fit into this?

In order for people to buy your products or services they need to know about you. Therefore you have to communicate with them in the most effective way possible. You can do this through a number of promotional tools. Some of these include:

- advertising
- direct mail
- press relations
- exhibitions
- seminars.

You can also do it through selling both on the telephone and face to face.

> **Selling, therefore, is one of the promotional tools available for you to target your prospects and convert them into customers.**

Selling to the right person

Many people make the mistake of selling to the wrong person. They waste time and energy, and in the process can also lose the sale. What you say to one person will almost invariably get misinterpreted when it is passed on to another. So you need to check at the beginning of a sales interview that you are talking to the right person. Before I look at how you do this I need to examine **'The Decision Making Unit'** or **'DMU'** as it is most commonly referred to.

Sometimes you may have to go through several people in one company before reaching the Decision Maker. This is particularly so in the capital equipment market and if the product or service you are selling is an expensive one. But even if you are selling to the consumer, a husband and wife perhaps, there is still a decision making unit involved, as we will see.

So who is in the Decision Making Unit?

This may contain some, or even, all of the following:

- **Gatekeepers**

Everyone knows the gatekeepers! These are the people who think they are paid to keep you out.

It never ceases to amaze me how some companies make it so difficult for people to approach them. They treat everyone with suspicion and constantly moan about sales people little realising that their organisation has sales people too and is in the business of selling.

You will more frequently come up against the Gatekeepers in telephone selling and if you are cold calling face to face. If you have an appointment though you should be able to get through these people without too much trouble.

- **Users**

These are people who may use the piece of machinery, the computer software, or the equipment or systems you are selling. They could therefore influence the purchasing decision by telling the main decision maker what they like and don't like about a product or a service and, of course, who they like and dislike! Those authorising the purchase may ask the Users for their opinion. Users could also have an effect on future sales and whether the goods or services purchased were actually value for money and worked satisfactorily.

- **Influencers**

These are sometimes more difficult to spot. They may not obviously be involved in the buying process but they may influence it. They could even be outsiders who have heard of your company and its reputation and either endorse it or slate it.

In a transaction affecting consumer goods one

partner may be buying a piece of equipment but the other partner may well effect the decision to buy even though he or she may not be a direct user of that product. For example they may not like the colour of the product, the company or the salesperson and could influence the buyer accordingly.

You may also find that your Gatekeeper is an Influencer i.e. the person on the security gate is the Managing Director's father. The receptionist is the Managing Director's wife. If they didn't like you then you could find yourself without a sale.

- **Buyers**

These are professional people within the organisation, a purchasing manager or buyer, whose job it is to source and buy on behalf of the business. They are paid to get the best deal so generally speaking they will be tough and thorough negotiators. They can often be the most difficult people to sell to because of this.

- **Deciders**

Who decides on whether to go ahead and buy? This can depend on the value of the transaction. Decisions to purchase may be taken lower down the line for low cost or routine purchases, a Secretary, Stores person or Manager, but are usually at top level where big money is involved so you may be talking to a Managing Director or a Financial or Production Director etc..

- **Specifiers**

These are often people like architects who may specify building materials; design engineers who may specify what type of components are needed for a specific project. Specifiers may have to be convinced at an early stage that a specification embracing your product will satisfy their requirements.

> **Finding the right person to sell to, or going through the various people in the Decision Making Unit, requires a methodical and persistent approach.**

So how do you know if the person you are seeing is the decision maker?

Simple - ask them - and ask them right at the beginning of the meeting.

For example:

'Would anyone else be involved in the decision to buy?'

Or

'Who else needs to be involved if you decide to go ahead?'

You will then find out if you need to involve

anyone else in the sales presentation at this stage, or if you have to return to make another sales presentation.

If the person you are seeing reveals that he/she is not the final decision maker, ask if the decision maker is available to join the meeting. If they are not available then continue with the sales interview. It would be impolite to terminate it so abruptly and you do not know how much influence the person you are seeing has with the decision maker. Try and determine this and adjust your sales pitch accordingly. Try and ensure before you leave that you make another appointment to return when you can see both the decision maker and anyone else involved in the buying decision.

Consumer selling

If you are in the business of selling to the consumer then don't think that the decision making unit doesn't apply, because it does.

For example how many car salespeople have got it wrong by selling only to the man in a transaction and ignoring the woman? They have underestimated the influence of the woman in the decision making unit.

I was involved in training some salespeople who work at the luxury end of the motorboat market. These boats retail for £250,000 upwards. Many of the buyers are men who quite often are accompanied by a female partner. Again, as with our car example, it would be wrong to ignore the influence of the woman in this relationship, as equally it would be wrong to ignore the influence of any children who might accompany them. Whilst you may not be directly selling to the woman or the children if you ignore their concerns and views then you could lose the sale.

Whilst it is always wrong to make assumptions we will nevertheless make one here and say that our man is looking for speed and performance from the motorboat whilst our woman is looking for comfort, spaciousness and interior design. We will, therefore, need to address the needs of both parties and sell the relevant benefits to the relevant person.

In summary

- The difference between selling and marketing is that marketing is a complete business philosophy. It means putting the customer at the centre of your business

- It involves you knowing your customers and communicating with them in the most effective way in order to win more business from them

- It is about understanding who your customers are and anticipating what they want, not just today or tomorrow, but next year, the year after, and so on

- In order for people to buy your products or

services they need to know about you

- You have to communicate with them in the most effective way possible

- You can do this through a number of promotional tools. Some of these include:

    advertising
    direct mail
    press relations
    exhibitions
    seminars.

- You can also do it through selling both on the telephone and face to face

- Selling is one of the promotional tools available for you to target your prospects and convert them into customers

- Many people make the mistake of selling to the wrong person. Check at the beginning of a sales interview that you are talking to the right person

- In some cases you may have to go through several people in one company before reaching the Decision Maker

- The Decision Making Unit may contain some, or even, all of the following:

Gatekeepers
Users
Influencers

**Buyers
Deciders
Specifiers**

- Finding the right person to sell to, or going through the various people in the Decision Making Unit, requires a methodical and persistent approach

- The decision making unit can also apply in the selling of consumer goods.

Chapter two

Understanding buyer behaviour

Understanding how buyers behave will give you greater knowledge in the sales process and therefore make you better equipped to convert the sale.

**People generally buy for two reasons:
Objective reasons
Subjective reasons.**

You will need to satisfy both.

What influences someone to buy?

Individuals will buy some products or services to satisfy the basic **physiological needs** i.e. to satisfy hunger and thirst, to be free from pain, injury, for security, safety reasons etc. or because they have to comply with the law. These are the **objective reasons** why people buy.

But it is not always simply a question of needing or wanting a product or service to serve a specific purpose or to satisfy that basic physiological need that stimulates an individual to buy. The buyer will also be asking other questions about that product and service. They will buy for **subjective reasons**.

These subjective reasons are personal based and are referred to as the **psychological reasons** involved in buying.

For example, if you are buying a car you need the car to get you from A to B, you may also need it to be a certain size to carry a certain number of individuals, these are the **objective reasons** for buying. But your decision to buy a particular model or make, or to buy from a particular garage, will also be based on subjective reasons.

The **subjective reasons or psychological reasons** could be:

- Will this car suit my lifestyle?

- Will it make me look good in the eyes of my peers or superiors?

- By buying this car what statement am I making and is that the right one for me?

- Does this car fit with my role as a director, father, mother, husband, wife etc..

Let me give you another example. I was working with a theatre whose box office staff had to sell tickets to group buyers. The group buyers want **good discounts** - the **objective reason** for buying. But the group buyer also wants to book a show that is popular and one that **everyone in his party will enjoy.** If he does he will come away basking in the warm glow of being credited with that success – this is the **subjective reason** for buying. So the box office staff has to satisfy the prospective buyer on both fronts; that he is getting a good deal and that his party will enjoy the show.

Whether it is a product or a service you are selling you need to understand why people buy - both the objective and subjective reasons.

The **subjective or psychological reasons for buying a product or a service** can be summed up as follows:

- to give pleasure

- to give a sense of satisfaction

- to feed and raise self esteem

- to satisfy and feed an ego

- to reinforce group identity - to give a sense of belonging

- to satisfy the need for power

- to satisfy the need for recognition

- to satisfy the need for approval

- to satisfy the need for respect.

Selling a Service

The difference between selling a product and a service is that you can see a product, you can touch it, even taste it sometimes, but a service is intangible. It cannot be seen, touched or tasted.

With a service it is the people who deliver it and therefore the maxim 'people buy people' is even more relevant and vital here.

For example, when people buy a legal service they are buying for the **objective reasons**, i.e. they need a lawyer to help them resolve a problem.

In choosing that lawyer they are also buying the **subjective reasons**. The lawyer (who is the salesperson in this instance) must demonstrate to the prospective client the following:

- an understanding of the client's situation

- the technical expertise to deal with the client's problem

- the ability to talk the language of the client

- the ability to provide an efficient service

- accessibility when the client wants it.

In addition to the lawyer the prospective client will also be buying:

- the reputation of the legal firm

- the image of the legal firm

- the staff in the firm and the way the telephone is answered etc.

- the speed of service

- specialist knowledge

- cost

- the personality of advisers

- the breadth of service available

- personal recommendation by peers.

So the legal firm must make sure it delivers all the above. If it fails to live up to the client's expectation then the client will be dissatisfied with the service and will tell other people, thereby damaging future sales for the firm. So you can see that there are many individuals involved in selling our legal firm.

With a service you are buying all the people who work for that organisation, their attitude, their personality and their level of expertise. My marketing and media clients are buying my professional expertise, my skills and knowledge as well as me as a person and the fact that they are able to get on with me.

So in order to sell a service you need to be both

personally acceptable and have expertise. In addition, in service selling the prospect is often buying an ongoing relationship. Selling a service, and particularly a professional service, is **highly personal.**

You may wish to return to this chapter after you have read chapters three and four. Then you will be able to draw up a list of both the objective and subjective reasons of why people will buy from you.

In summary

- Understanding how buyers behave will give you greater knowledge in the sales process and therefore make you better equipped to convert the sale

- Individuals will buy products or services to satisfy the basic physiological needs. These are the **objective reasons why people buy**

- Individuals will also be looking to satisfy the psychological needs. These are the **subjective reasons**

- An individual could be asking whether the product or service:

    Suits his lifestyle?

    Makes him look good in the eyes of his peers or superiors?

Fits with his role as director, father, mother, husband, wife etc..

- When selling a service the maxim 'people buy people' is even more relevant and vital

- In order to sell a service you need to be both personally acceptable and have expertise

- Selling a service and particularly a professional service is **highly personal.**

Chapter three

Understanding Buying Motivations

In my book *The Easy Step by Step Guide to Telemarketing, Cold Calling & Appointment Making* I looked at the buying motivations because we are selling over the telephone. We also need to look at them here, when we are selling face to face.

When people buy they always ask 'why should I?' 'What's in it for me?' You need to be able to satisfy those questions if you are going to secure the sale and come away with the business.

> **There are two sets of buying motivations:**
>
> **Positive and Negative.**

It is always best to assume that most people you will be selling to will have the negative buying motivations in their minds - the 'why should I - what's in it for me?' syndrome. In order to win their business you will need to switch them over to the positive buying motivations. So how do you do this?

Let's take a look at the buying motivations and understand them.

The negative buying motivations

When you meet someone trying to sell you something your reaction can be summed up as follows:

- I don't trust you

- I don't need you

- No, I don't think you can help me

- I'm in no hurry to buy - I'll think about it. I'll get back to you

- No, I don't think you can help me.

This could be what your prospective customer is thinking.

If you don't switch that person over to the positive buying motivations you will have lost the sale.

Think about this situation:

You answer a knock on your front door. When you open it a stranger is standing on the doorstep with a holdall trying to sell something to you. You look at him/her. What is going through your mind? Is it something along the lines of

'Who is this person? What do they want?' You're not sure about them. The negative buying motivations are very much uppermost in your mind.

When someone comes to your home or office to sell you something you are looking for reasons not to buy rather than reasons to buy.

You are wary, sceptical, and hesitant. If that sales person doesn't gain your confidence at the beginning of the transaction then they never will and the sale will be lost. So how do you prevent this happening to you when selling?

Positive buying motivations

You need to switch your prospective customer over to the positive buying motivations. These are as follows:

- I am important

- Consider my needs

- Will your ideas help me?

- What are the details?

- What are the problems?

- I approve.

You get the sale.

Then there is a final stage you'd do well to remember:

- **Remember I am still important.**

It is important having won the business to reassure the customer that he or she has made the right choice. You also need to ensure that your after care/customer care is working. If you fail to look after your customer then all the effort made by the marketing team, production and the sales person will be wasted. And remember it costs eight times as much to win a new customer as it does to retain an existing one.

Switching from negative to positive

So how do you switch your prospect from the negative buying motivations to the positive buying motivations?

The first two stages in the positive buying motivation process are crucial:

- **I am important**
- **Consider my needs**

Here are some ways of making the individual feel important:

- **address them by their correct name and title.**

You need to judge this accurately. I know sales people who have lost the sale by being too familiar and addressing someone by their first name when they should have used the surname and their title. So how do you know how to address them?

The simple rule is how they introduce themselves to you. If they introduce themselves as John Smith then you can use their first name. If they introduce themselves as Mr. Smith it's Mr. Smith and the same goes for women using the first name or Mrs., Miss or Ms as appropriate. If in doubt err on the side of formal rather than the informal first name usage and let them invite you to call them by their first name.

Another general rule to take into consideration is their age and their position in the organisation. If the prospect is older than me, or very senior in the organisation, I would be more formal in addressing them. In addition, you may find some organisations are traditionally more formal in their approach than others, the professions for example.

- **Use the persons name in your conversation, particularly at the beginning of the sales interview.**

I find this also helps me to remember someone's name.

- **Listen throughout the whole of the sales process and I mean really listen.**

Listening is the highest form of courtesy.

There are two types of listening:

social or casual
critical or analytical.

It is the latter form of listening you need to do. You need to assimilate what the prospect is saying, understand it, interpret it and store it possibly for retrieval later. Listening well is an extremely difficult skill and takes practice. Often sales people are too busy thinking of what they are going to say next to really listen.

- **Ask the right questions to find out what they need.**

The good salesperson needs to ask the right questions to get the prospective customer to open up. He or she therefore has to ask what are called 'open questions.' I look at listening skills and questioning techniques in more detail in chapter seven.

So how else do you get your prospective customer to switch over to the first two positive buying motivations?

I am important
Consider my needs.

It can be fairly easy if you remember the following:

> **People like to talk about two things, themselves - and if they're in business, their company.**

So you need to get your prospect talking. It is as simple as that. If you, as the salesperson, are doing most of the talking during the sales interview then you are losing it. Get control back, ask a question, shut up and listen to the answer. Again, I will cover what questions to ask in a later chapter.

Here is another way you can make your prospect feel important:

- **Demonstrate that you have prepared for the sales interview.**

You could refer to something early in your conversation with the prospect to demonstrate that you have taken the time and trouble to research their business.

Having switched the prospect over to the first two positive buying motivations you will then need to take the others into consideration. These are:

- **Will your ideas help me?**
- **What are the details?**
- **What are the problems?**
- **I approve.**

We will look at how we do this in chapters seven, eight and nine.

In summary

- The successful salesperson needs to satisfy the questions in the prospect's mind: 'Why should I?' 'What's in it for me?'

- There are two sets of buying motivations:

    Positive and Negative.

- In order to win business you will need to switch the prospective customer over to the positive buying motivations.

- Make your prospects feel important by:

    addressing them by their correct name and title

    using their name in your conversation, particularly at the beginning of the sales interview

    listening to them throughout the whole of the sales process

    asking them the right questions to find out what they need

    demonstrating that you have prepared for the sales interview

Chapter four

Know your product/service

In order to be an effective salesperson you need to have good product knowledge. This may sound a bit obvious but believe me I have come across many sales people in my time, both on my training courses and personally, who do not have nearly enough product knowledge. I am sure you have met them yourself.

For example just think of how many shops you have been into and asked a sales person for some information on a certain product and they have been unable to help you.

It is not enough though simply to know the product or service features but you will also need to know the benefits of those features because, as we examined in the previous chapter, people buy benefits not features. They want to know how your product or service will help them.

So let's take a look at this.

Features and Benefits

You need to examine this on two levels: firstly your company level and secondly an individual product/service level.

Why a company level? Well to be able to answer the question 'Why should I buy from your company rather than ABC Limited down the road?' In addition, prospects will want to know what makes your company different?

So take a long hard look at your business and what it provides.

Often when I go into companies to help them with their marketing and sales strategy I ask them the following question:

'Why should I buy from you?'

The directors will start rattling off a hundred and one reasons, all features, ending with a variation along the lines of 'and we're really nice people!'

Nice you may be, and of course, as I said earlier, people need to like you in order to buy from you, but nice isn't enough for someone to part with their hard earned cash or their company's money. They need to be able to see the benefits.

What you are selling can fall into one or more of the following categories:

- **the solution to a problem they have**

- **something that will fulfill a need in them or their company**

- **something that will make them happier or feel good**

- **something that will make their business**

more efficient i.e. in that it will save them time and/or money, or make them more profitable, win them more business etc..

Remember the objective and the subjective reasons we examined in chapter two? In order for people to see that the 'something' you are selling will fulfill one or more of the items listed above they need to be told what the benefits of buying that product or service will give them.

Let's look at some examples starting at the company level.

Feature
A feature of a company may be that it has easy access from the motorway.

So what? Are you going to wait for the prospect to make the leap in his/her mind of what that will mean to him/her? No, you are not, you are going to tell them that **it means** they will be able to reach your warehouse, factory, shop, office easily and quickly without any hassle of fighting through the traffic in the town. That is the **benefit.**

Feature
Another feature may be that you have car parking.

The **benefit** of that feature is simple for all to see but you need to reinforce it to your prospect:

For example:

'**Which means** Mr. Jones you won't have to

waste time driving around trying to find somewhere to park. What's more our parking is free so you won't have to pay, or hunt for change for the meter either.'

I have strengthened the benefit by adding another one i.e. the free parking. Then I can further strengthen it by saying:

'So to sum up you can reach us quickly and simply and hassle free.'

Can you see how much stronger I have made this feature by stressing the benefits?

But you may be asking why do I have to say these things? The prospect isn't stupid. Well, you need to say them for two reasons:

1. The prospect may not be able to make the leap between the feature and the benefit and by spelling it out you are helping them.

2. If the prospect has made the leap between the feature and the benefit then by saying aloud what is going through the prospect's mind you are strengthening the point.

This helps to build a **buying signal**. Your prospect may be sitting in front of you nodding his/her head, or saying, 'really!' or raising his/her eyebrows, sitting forward in his/her seat, all of which show interest - these are buying signals. If this happens little light bulbs should be flashing in your head. You have a buying signal so capitalise on it by repeating and strengthening it and adding in another relevant benefit.

For example:

'Yes we do have ample parking Mr. Jones and we're open until 6pm every day, or we can deliver to you. Which would be the more convenient?'

I'm now **closing** as well. But I get ahead of myself. I will come back to this point in chapter nine.

If you are not looking and listening you will miss these vital buying signals. Many people do.

So to return to our features and benefits.

Feature
Another feature may be something along the lines of: 'We're a well established company.'

The **benefit** of this is that we have a track record of dealing with this type of work. We have an established reputation in this field. What you are in fact saying is that your company is reliable and trustworthy.

Feature
'We have a very comprehensive product range.'

The **benefit** of this means that we have something to suit all tastes and budgets and availability is not a problem.

> **The two magic words (as I call them) which turn a feature into a benefit are 'which means.'**

Here are some exercises for you to do:

1. Write out a list of features and benefits for your company. List the features and then say to yourself 'which means.' Then add the benefit. Remember it is benefits that sell not features on their own.

2. Now do this exercise for every product or service you provide. What are the features and benefits of a particular product/service? Know them inside out and back to front. Be prepared before you go out to see a prospect.

3. You may also wish to return to chapter two. Re-read it and then draw up a list of the objective and subjective reasons of why people will buy your products/services.

In summary

- In order to be an effective salesperson you need to have product knowledge

- You need to know the features of what you are offering and the benefits of those features

- You need to examine this on two levels: firstly your company level and secondly an individual product/service level

- Prospects will want to know what makes your company different. Why they should buy from you?

- What you are selling is one or more of the following:

    the solution to a problem

    something that will fulfill a need

    something that will make someone happier or feel good

    something that will make a business more efficient or life easier and more enjoyable .

- The two magic words which turn a feature into a benefit are the words 'which means.'

Chapter five

Know your market place and your competitors

Effective selling means knowing who else is in your market and what they are selling. Why? Because, as we examined in the last chapter, one of the objections you might need to handle in the sales interview could be 'Why should I buy from you and not one of your competitors?'

You will need to have some idea of the size of your market. Of who else is operating in it and what they are providing. In addition, you will need to have some idea of where you are positioned in relation to them.

Here is an exercise for you to do. See if you can answer all the questions listed.

1. List five of your competitors in one of your main product or service areas.

2. What are their strengths?

3. What are their weaknesses?

4. Where are you positioned in relation to them?

5. What makes you better than or different from your competitors?

How did you get on? It is not always easy to answer these questions as the market place continually changes. New competitors will enter your market; your customers' requirements will change. You need to keep abreast of this and adapt your products/services, or the way they are delivered, to suit changing expectations. Make sure you continually research your market place and customer requirements.

Getting ready for the sales interview

All of the above forms part of the preparation for the sales interview. Of course you may not always be going out to visit your prospective customers, your prospects may visit your premises, or you may be selling at an exhibition where prospects come on to your stand. In all of these cases you should do your pre sales research.

Pre sales research

This means having knowledge of your products/services, the features and benefits of those products/services and both the objective and subjective reasons why people buy your products/services.

You also need to have knowledge of your market place, your competitors and what they provide.

An understanding and knowledge of your prospect's needs and wants will be built up through your own experience or by talking to those who work with you who may have greater knowledge than you.

You should also read trade journals, professional magazines etc. to have an increased awareness of what is happening in your prospect's marketplace. For example if you are selling boats to consumers then you will not only need to know about your own products but about the market place in general and have a good picture of the sort of person who buys your type of boat, their lifestyle, socio economic background etc..

If you are in business-to-business selling do you have any press items about the prospect you are visiting that may help you in the sales interview? You may also wish to carry out a company search before hand to find out a little more about the prospect's business and check its credit rating.

Set your objectives

What do you want to achieve from the sales interview? Will you be able to get the order at the first interview? This may depend on what you are selling. Capital equipment sales often take longer to convert and require more than one sales visit as does selling some services.

In addition, if you remember back to our Decision Making Unit in chapter one, you may find that you need to sell to more than one person and therefore the whole selling process will take longer. You may need to return to the company to demonstrate equipment or to give a presentation.

If the purchase is an expensive one, say a luxury yacht, or capital equipment, then the prospect may take longer to make a decision.

You may wish to obtain more information about the prospect from this first visit and leave the door open to go back in later.

Check your presentation material

Do you have the necessary leaflets, price lists and brochures to hand? What does your company literature look like? Is it old and outdated and therefore reflecting badly on the image of the company? Or is it up to date and reflects a good corporate image that suits the type of customers you have?

If selling at an exhibition do you have all the necessary material and equipment on display? What does your stand look like? Is it friendly and welcoming?

Prepare as well as you can before any sales

interview. Respect the saying:

> **To fail to prepare is to prepare to fail!**

In summary

- Do your pre sales research

- Have knowledge of your market place, your competitors and what they provide

- An understanding and knowledge of your prospect's needs and wants will be built up through your experience or by talking to those who work with you who may have greater knowledge than you

- You should also read trade journals, professional magazines etc. to have an increased awareness of what is happening in your prospect's marketplace

- If you are in business-to-business selling do you have any press items about the prospect you are visiting that may help you in the sales interview?

- You may also wish to carry out a company search before hand to find out a little more about the prospect's business and check its credit rating

- Set your objectives - what do you want to achieve from the sales interview? Will you be able to get the order at the first interview?

- Some sales take longer to convert and require more than one sales visit as does selling some services

- You may find that you need to sell to more than one person and therefore the whole selling process will take longer

- You may need to return to the company to demonstrate equipment or give a presentation

- If the purchase is an expensive one, the prospect may take longer to make a decision

- You may wish to obtain more information about the prospect from this first visit and leave the door open to go back in later

- Check your presentation material - do you have the necessary leaflets, price lists and brochures to hand?

- Prepare as well as you can before any sales interview.

Chapter six

The Sales Interview - Approach

The selling structure I am giving you is called **A.D.D.I.N.** By using this I hope you will **add in** your product or service to the prospective clients business, home or lifestyle.

It stands for:

- **Approach**
- **Discussion**
- **Diagnosis**
- **Interpretation**
- **Needs**

We are going to look at the first phase of the sales interview. **Approach.**

Approach

If you are visiting a company to make a sale then always ensure you arrive early. Sit (or better still stand - it aids authority and gives energy) in reception. Here you can glean a great deal about an organisation.

What do the premises look like? Are they falling to pieces? If so how healthy is that business's finances and therefore its ability to pay you?

How well are you greeted? Is the receptionist

friendly and welcoming or hostile? What does this tell you about the company?

Receptions are gossip zones. They shouldn't be if the company is switched on but in my experience many businesses neglect this vital area. This is good news for the sales person because he/she can find out about the company from eavesdropping on the gossip. Obviously if the receptionist is moaning about redundancies I would question the ability of the company to pay you!

You may also learn something about the person you are going to visit. In my book, **The Easy Step by Step Guide to Marketing,** I quote the experience I had when I was visiting a large multinational organisation in Surrey. I was due to see the Commercial Director, in this instance to sell in my training services. The two women on reception decided to undertake a character assassination on the man I was visiting. I learnt an awful lot about him in those few minutes, not all of it true I am sure, but it gave me some insight into the nature of the person I was about to visit and some clues on how to approach the interview! I did win the contract, which was worth quite a considerable amount.

At reception take a look at the literature that is lying around on the tables. Do the company have a press cuttings file, or a company newsletter? This could give you valuable information and you may be able to refer to it in your conversation with the prospect to demonstrate you are interested in them.

What awards are on display on the walls and what does this tell you about the company?

Also don't forget the gatekeeper - the receptionist. Take time to be pleasant to him/her and ask gentle questions about the business if you can but don't pry too deeply. Keep the conversation light and friendly. Plus this receptionist may very well be related to the person you are visiting and therefore be an influencer, so don't pass any comments you might regret later.

If the prospect is visiting you at your premises or coming on to your exhibition stand how welcoming are your premises or your stand and how welcoming are you?

Let's take a look at the **Approach** in more detail.

If I was to ask you the question, 'When do you close the sale?' What would be your answer? Well, the correct answer is you begin to close the sale the first few seconds you meet the prospect.

> **You never get a second chance to make a first impression.**

When you meet someone they will sum you up in the first five seconds. They will be taking into consideration your appearance, your body language and the way you speak. So ensure you get these right. A first impression can be a lasting impression and you could lose that sale in the first few seconds.

Your appearance

Many people overlook this important aspect and whilst you can't possibly know the prospect's tastes in clothing and grooming you can eliminate some mistakes by following some very simple guidelines.

Make sure your shoes are clean and not falling to pieces. I have sat in on a number of sales presentations with clients, or on interviews, and have heard the decision maker comment on the state of someone's shoes.

For men your trousers should not be too long and hanging over your shoes. Neither should they be flying at half-mast displaying Mickey Mouse socks or, worse, white socks. You may like them and they may be fine in certain situations but not if you want to win this business. I once saw a man dressed in a very dark sombre suit wearing bright pink socks and grey shoes!! I am afraid his credibility was completely blown.

If you are wearing trousers that have belt loops please wear a belt and one that matches the trousers. This applies to both males and females. Again ensure the trousers sit comfortably on you and that they are not torn in any way. Yes, I have seen a man with trousers torn at the crutch!!

If you are rather stout make sure your clothes fit you and that your shirt or blouse is not straining across your midriff. Also, if wearing a jacket, make sure it fits when fastened.

If a man is wearing a tie it should be knotted neatly. It is not always necessary in some industries to wear a tie and an open necked shirt and even a casual polo shirt is acceptable. Only you know who you are visiting and what they would be expecting.

> **The golden rule is:**
> **Where I am going?**
> **Who am I seeing?**
> **What do I wear?**

If you dress too inappropriately you will alienate your prospect. 55% of the impression you give out is based on your appearance and your body language so take time to get this right.

- **Good grooming is essential**.

Your hair should be clean and there should be no tell tale dandruff signs on your collar. And don't overdo the aftershave if you are a man or perfume if you are a woman. I know women decision makers who have taken an instant dislike to a man because of his overpowering aftershave, it can be the same for men with women wearing strong perfume.

Obviously check your breath. A good way to know if you suffer from bad breath is to lick the inside of your wrist, wait for five seconds then sniff it. This will tell you. Or visit a dentist and ask his or her professional advice. Having bad breath, like having a bad body odour, is something even your best friends won't tell you. It is so personal and delicate and yet something can be done about both.

For women there are some additional rules. Whereas men have a sort of uniform – jacket, shirt and trousers, women have a much greater choice when it comes to what to wear. The basic rule is the more flesh you show the less credible you will be. You need to look professional and competent, not as if you are about to go to the beach or nightclub. Alright, so some male buyers might be impressed and persuaded by a flash of leg and a glimpse of cleavage but we're talking different tactics here and I will leave these to your imagination!

- **The group sales presentation.**

If you are giving a sales presentation to a group of people then you need to project authority. If you are a woman then dress classic rather than too fussy. Darker suits aid authority and you can combine this with a striking necklace or scarf.

For both men and women check the fit of the suit when buttoned. When presenting formally always stand and make sure your jacket is buttoned up.

Your body language.

55% of the impression you give out is through your appearance and body language so you also need to examine the way you greet the prospect.

Walk forwards with your arm outstretched, not too stiff but with your elbow tucked into your waist and ladies always offer your hand first. Because the handshake is not a normal form of greeting for women many men are not sure whether to shake hands or not. If a woman offers her hand first then any hesitation will be removed from the prospect's mind. I have only ever had my hand refused once by a man, when I was being introduced as the marketing consultant in an accountancy firm. It told me an awful lot about that man and his manner towards me. After talking to him for a while I offered my hand again on leaving and that time he took it, so hopefully I had persuaded him that I wasn't a complete waste of time and money!

As you shake hands with the prospect smile at him or her and give him or her good eye contact.

Your handshake should be firm and dry. Again it is not always easy to know if you are giving a good handshake, as people won't tell you. On my courses I shake hands with everyone and I get delegates to shake hands with each other and tell each other honestly what their handshake is like. I will often ask someone to firm it up.

Don't do the double clutch handshake. This is often referred to as the Politicians Handshake. This is where someone takes your hand in both of theirs. It is done to try and reassure you that they are on your side. It is also often interpreted as being patronising. People who have a dominant personality use it in the main. More about this in chapter eleven.

Women should practice what I call the man's handshake; they should take the whole hand and not just the fingertips. A good firm confident grip gives the impression you are confident (even if you're not.)

Only when invited, sit down and not before. Keep your body language open and sit back in the chair. Do not put anything on the prospect's desk or table without asking first. The desk or table is their territory and you are invading it without permission if you don't ask.

Set the tone - opening the conversation

You will also need to set the tone for the sales interview. Open the conversation with neutral remarks. This can include comments on the traffic, the weather etc.. Or you can compliment them on their directions, their building, their receptionist, and the awards displayed on the wall in reception before moving into the sales presentation and the area of **Discussion.**

At an Exhibition

Before we move onto the next stage in our sales structure it is worth mentioning a few additional points on selling at an exhibition.

For a start never sit on your stand and wait for people to come up to you, they won't. People are wary and reluctant to open conversations, so you need to do it. Give them good eye contact, smile and open the conversation gently, a neutral comment can be best.

Always start with an **open question** rather than a closed one. I cover this in detail in the next chapter but ask them '**how**' they are enjoying the exhibition rather than '**are**' they enjoying the exhibition.

Never stand at the front of your exhibition unit with your arms folded – you will look like a police officer guarding the entrance and no one will approach you. And don't patrol the entrance to your stand either, walking up and down in front of it. Move out slightly into the aisle and be welcoming.

If you have something moving on your stand, or something of interest on display, this can help capture on-lookers and then you can start talking to them. All the sales points covered in this book apply to selling at an exhibition.

In summary

- By using the sales structure **A.D.D.I.N.** you will add in your product or service to the prospective client's business, home or lifestyle

- **A.D.D.I.N.** stands for:

    Approach
    Discussion
    Diagnosis
    Interpretation
    Needs

- Arrive early for an appointment if you are visiting a company and see what you can glean about that organisation in reception

- Take time to be pleasant to the receptionist

- If the prospect is visiting you at your premises, or coming on to your exhibition stand, how welcoming are your premises or your stand and how welcoming are you?

- You begin to close the sale the first few seconds you meet the prospect

- You never get a second chance to make a first impression so make sure yours is right

- Make sure your shoes are clean and not falling to pieces

- Trousers should not be too long and hanging over your shoes. Neither should they be flying at half-mast displaying Mickey Mouse socks or, worse, white socks

- If you are wearing trousers that have belt loops wear a belt and one that matches the trousers

- If you are wearing a tie it should be knotted neatly

- The golden rule is: Where I am going? Who am I seeing? What do I wear?

- If you dress too inappropriately you will alienate your prospect

- 55% of the impression you make on other people is based on your appearance and your body language so take time to get this right

- Don't overdo the aftershave if you are a man or perfume if you are a woman.

- For women the basic rule is the more flesh you show the less credible you will be. You need to look professional and competent

- If you are giving a group sales presentation you need to project authority

- In greeting the prospect walk forwards with your arm outstretched, not too stiff but with your elbow tucked into your waist, smile and give good eye contact

- Your handshake should be firm and dry. Don't do the double clutch handshake. It is often interpreted as being patronising

- Women should practice what I call the man's handshake; they should take the whole hand and not just the fingertips

- Only when invited, sit down and not before. Keep your body language open and sit back in the chair. Do not put anything on the prospect's desk or table without asking. The desk or table is their territory and you are invading it without permission if you don't ask

- Set the tone for the sales interview by starting with neutral remarks.

Chapter seven

The Sales Interview – Discussion, Diagnose Interpretation and Need

If you remember back to the buying motivations discussed in chapter three you will recall the first two positive buying motivations:

- **I am important**
- **Consider my needs.**

In order to make people feel important we need to get them to talk, to open up, and we need to listen and interpret what they are saying. Only by doing this will we be able to identify their reasons for buying, their needs and **add in** our product to satisfy those needs.

So the next stage of our sales structure is to stimulate discussion.

Discussion

We stimulate discussion by asking the right kind of questions – **open questions.** These are designed to get the prospect to open up.

But first let me give you a don't - **Don't ever hand your literature to a prospect at the beginning of the sale.** This will guarantee that he or she will be looking at it and not listening to you or wanting to participate in the discussion. Save your literature until the end of the sales process or at the interpretation stage.

Open Questions

Asking open questions will help you to:

- properly understand what it is the prospect wants

- make the prospect feel important

- find out how the prospect feels about you and your organisation

- control the conversation

- understand the prospect's needs.

Open questions are questions that can't be answered with a single 'yes' or 'no.' They begin with the following words as highlighted in the box below.

> **OPEN QUESTIONS**
> **What**
> **Who**
> **Where**
> **When**
> **Why**
> **How**

So you might be saying 'Easy. I ask these all the time', but I could wager with you now that you most probably don't and that you are asking 'closed' questions instead.

Closed Questions

Closed questions are questions that you will quite often get a simple 'yes' or 'no' answer. They begin with the following words highlighted in the box below.

> **CLOSED QUESTIONS**
>
> **Is/Are
> Has/Have
> Can/Could
> Shall/Should
> Do/Did
> Will/Would.**

If you ask 'closed' questions, you will make life a lot harder for yourself, particularly with an individual who is not naturally forthcoming, or is hostile. Asking closed questions will force you to ask two questions instead of one, as you can with open questions.

For example:

Closed Question: 'Did you go out last night?'

Answer: 'Yes.'

Open Question: 'Where did you go?'

I have had to ask two questions instead of one. I could simply have asked:

'Where did you go last night?' or

'What did you do last night?'

When you were three years old you were extremely skilled at asking these open questions. Those of you who have young children or nephews, nieces, grandchildren, know this. Children can drive you round the bend with their constant questioning but it is how they learn. We did the same years ago but as we grew up we were probably told not to ask so many questions, not to pry. Consequently we became too embarrassed to ask and then too lazy to probe and more interested in what we had to say about ourselves than asking others about themselves. So we need to relearn this lost art. Like any other art the only way to become good at it is by practice. We need to learn to ask an open question and then listen to the answer. We need to learn to probe gently.

Open Situation Questions

So in order to **stimulate discussion** we need to ask **open situation questions**. These are questions that are designed to probe the prospect's situation. For example:

- How many staff do you employ?

- What sort of markets do you operate in?

- Where do you currently export?

If we take our **theatre example** used earlier, where we were selling box office tickets to group bookers, we can ask:

- What sort of shows does your group enjoy?

- How often does your group attend shows during the year?

- How many of you are there?

- What sort of age mix is in your group?

If we take our **luxury motorboat example** we can ask:

- How are you intending to use the boat?

- Where do you usually motor?

- What arrangements have you made to moor the boat?

- How many people does it need to accommodate?

If I were selling my **training services** to a prospect I would ask the following open situation questions:

- How many people are you looking at training?

- What are their positions in your company?

- What are you hoping to achieve by the training?

- Where are you thinking of holding the training session?

From all the above examples you will get information.

> **You cannot sell your product or service until you have information. Miss out this vital first stage and you will miss the sale!**

The sales person who starts by giving his or her sales spiel will surely fail. It is not enough to tell the prospect who you are and what you have and then invite them to buy, the prospect needs to feel important, they need to know that you have considered their needs, they also need to see the benefits of buying from you and your company.

Of course you may be put under extreme pressure by your prospect. The prospect may be giving you an interview rather grudgingly and remember those negative buying motivations, the prospect could be highly sceptical and suspicious of you and your company. The prospect may very well start the sales interview by saying something along the lines of:

'So come on then sell to me.'

Or

'I can only give you ten minutes so what do you do?'

Or

'What are you going to sell me?'

In these, and similar cases, your instinct could very well be to let your sales spiel come out. Having finished it you then sit back and say, 'So are you interested?' to which the prospect replies, 'No thanks,' or 'I'll think about it.'

So curb that instinct, instead throw the ball back into the prospect's court. For example:

Salesperson: 'Of course I will be delighted to tell you what we do but first, so that I can find out how I can help you, I need to ask you a few questions. Tell me **what** sort of training have you carried out in the past?'

I am into my **open situation questions** and getting the discussion going. Even if the prospect is reluctant to begin with he or she will soon warm up once they are talking about themselves or their company. You will need to chip in with a few more open questions to keep the discussion going and of course at the same time listen avidly and critically.

I am not saying you should never use closed questions. They have their place. They can be used to obtain clarification or to elicit a specific response.

For example: 'Is it raining?' This will get you a 'yes' or 'no' answer. It may be all the information you need to help you decide whether or not to take an umbrella with you. Whereas if you were to ask 'What's the weather like?' you are likely to get a full blown weather forecast with the outlook for the next day and a comparison with the day before. You may not need or want all this information.

Closed questions can also be helpful in shutting someone down who talks too much without actually saying anything.

Let's just take a pause here because there are one or two things you need to be aware of in the questioning and listening arena before we move on.

- **Beware of asking multiple questions.**

This is where you roll several questions into one.

For example, 'How many people do you train Mr. Jones and how often do you train them?'

Which question is my prospect likely to answer - the first or the last? Will I have got all the information I need? No!

> **So ask an open question, shut up and wait for the answer.**

Resist the temptation to jump in and help them out, particularly if the prospect is a fairly slow individual and you are a rather quick and impatient one.

- **Beware of using value-loaded questions.**

This is where you load your values onto the other person. For example, 'So, what do you think of these thick union reps?' You might get the answer, 'I am one.'

- **Be careful of how and where you ask leading questions.**

Leading questions can be used in some circumstances where you want to lead the prospect into giving a positive response but it can work against you so you need to be careful.

For example if you say, 'You don't think this will work then?' you are likely to get the answer 'No.'

But leading questions can be used to close.

For example, 'Shall I go ahead and place the order then?' Or 'You'll agree to present this idea to your Directors then?' Hopefully they will say 'Yes.'

> **Ask the right questions. Open ones to get people to open up and give you information.**

Diagnose

We are now on to the **'Consider my needs'** part of the positive buying motivations. Here you will need to ask **problems and needs questions**. You will need to probe.

These questions (again open ones) are about probing the prospect's problems, difficulties or dissatisfactions with the existing situation.

For example:

'How satisfied were you with the work carried out?'

'What problems did you experience?'

You can use comparative questions to help you with this stage.

Comparative questions

This is a variation on the theme of open questions but comparative questions can give you yet more information and can help you explore different angles.

For example:

'How does this compare with the previous/current model?'

'How do these proposals compare to those outlined in your letter?'

These questions can often be followed up by more open probing questions.

Let's take a hypothetical sales interview:

Salesperson: 'How do our prices compare to what you are currently paying?'

Prospect: 'Your prices compare very favourably indeed.'

Salesperson: 'In what way?' **(Probing open question.)**

This may elicit for you yet more information along the lines of:

Prospect: ' Well although you are dearer I am not getting the level of service from my current suppliers that you say you can provide.'

Salesperson: 'And this high level of service is important to you?' **(Leading question.)**

Prospect: 'Yes.'

Salesperson: 'Why is that particularly?' **(Open probing question.)**

Prospect: 'Because we need our suppliers to respond to us rapidly. We can't afford to have the computer system down because that affects our performance and we lose sales as a result.'

From this discussion I can now diagnose what the prospect is buying and I can interpret the prospect's need.

Interpretation and Needs

The prospect has given me the details of his problem, what he is looking for from a supplier and the benefits he is buying. He is buying on service and he needs a speedy responsive service. He has also given me the implications of his problem - that he will lose business if his computer system stays down for too long.

I can now use another necessary skill in the sales process, that of **summarising** or reflecting as it is sometimes called. This helps the prospect to see that I have listened to him/her and that I have interpreted and understood his/her situation.

Salesperson: 'So what you **need** is a rapid response to any queries or problems you have and that if the system goes down a back up will be put in place that will minimise down time.'
(summarising skills – to show I have interpreted his needs.)

Prospect. 'Yes.'

Salesperson: 'Because we provide a 24 hour service we can give you round the clock support and back up, thereby minimising any downtime and ensuring you don't lose sales. What's more we can also guarantee an engineer will be with you within two hours.' **(I have sold in the relevant feature and benefit and I have strengthened it with a further benefit.)**

So both in the previous chapter and in this chapter I have used the sales process **A.D.D.I.N.**

Approach
Discussion
Diagnosis
Interpretation
Needs

To sum up, the essential ingredients for a successful selling process are:

- Make sure you are well prepared

- Get your appearance and opening body language right

- Ask open questions

- Don't be afraid to probe - ask 'why' and 'what do you mean?' Get the prospect to explain

- Use summarising skills to demonstrate to the prospect that you have understood and interpreted his/ her needs correctly

- Listen to what is being said.

So, finally in this chapter, I need to examine listening skills, an essential part in the sales process.

Listening actively

Listening, really listening, is the hardest thing to do and the highest form of courtesy! It is another part of the lost art of conversation. We are all so busy waiting to get our say in, to talk about our experiences, and ourselves that we don't really listen.

Listening well is vitally important in the sales structure. You have to listen not only to the words themselves (what people are saying), but the meaning behind the words. You have to pick up on the buying signals that can come through like: 'Oh!' or 'really' or a shift in body language position, as these will show interest in what you have just said. Once you have received and recognised a buying signal you will need to capitalise on it by focusing on the feature and benefit the prospect has picked up on and then strengthen it. You can even possibly go on to close after it.

As I mentioned in chapter three there are two types of listening:

- Social or casual

- Critical or analytical.

Social or casual listening is where we are only paying partial attention, some of what the other person is saying is going in, and the rest you are switching off or filtering away.

Critical listening is where you are really working hard to listen. You are receiving what is being said, you are analysing it, storing some information away in your head for later and thinking of what to ask next. Something of what you have stored away may then need to be retrieved later. If you are really listening, in the critical sense, you will find that your head aches and buzzes with it.

Unfortunately we are all becoming less adept at listening. As more and more of our stimulus is visual e.g. television, computers, the skill of listening gets harder for us. So here are some tips to help you listen more critically.

How to listen critically

- Train yourself to start listening with the first word and then listen intently

- Turn off all negative thoughts you have about the person talking

- Think at the speed they are talking; don't jump ahead

- Do not interrupt. When you are having a conversation with someone receive what he or she has said before rushing in with your contribution. If you feel you want to interrupt, think about pausing, and take a breath before you start to talk

- Ask questions once they have finished talking to probe their feelings, reactions, or get more details

- Use their name and use 'you' in conversation

- Use positive body language. Lean towards them

- Use open gestures

- Use good eye contact.

> **Listening and understanding are two of the key skills you need for successful selling.**

The sales interview summarised

Approach

> Introduction
> Check your appearance and body language
> Set the tone by making general opening remarks.

Discussion

>Ask open situation questions to stimulate discussion.

Diagnose

>Ask open problem questions - try to uncover their needs.
>Use comparative questions.

Interpretation

>Use summarising skills to show you have understood and interpreted the implications of their problems and identified with their needs.

Needs

>Tell them what they need by selling in the relevant feature and benefit which will help them to solve their problems/fulfill their needs.

Having done the above you will then need to close the sale i.e. ask for the business. Once having got it you should change the subject, shut up and get out. I will examine this in the next chapter.

A.D.D.I.N.

Add in your product or service to help the prospect improve his or her business, solve a problem or fulfill a need.

In summary

- In order to make people feel important we need to get them to talk, to open up, and we need to listen and interpret what they are saying

- We need to stimulate discussion by asking **open questions**

- Open questions are questions that can't be answered with a single 'yes' or 'no.'

- Open questions begin with: who, what, where, when, how and why

- **Closed questions** are questions that you will quite often get a simple 'yes' or 'no' answer

- Closed questions begin with: is/are, shall/should, have/has, will/would, do/did, can/could

- If you ask 'closed' questions, you will make life a lot harder for yourself, particularly with an individual who is not naturally forthcoming, or who is hostile.

- In order to **stimulate discussion** we need to ask **open situation questions**. These are questions that are designed to probe the prospect's situation

- You cannot sell in your product or service until you have information. Miss this vital first stage and you will miss the sale!

- Beware of asking multiple questions

- Beware of using value-loaded questions

- Be careful of how and where you ask leading questions

- To diagnose a prospect's needs you will need to ask problems and needs questions. You will need to probe. You can use comparative questions to help you with this stage

- **Comparative questions** can give you more information and can help you explore different angles

- **Summarising** skills enable the prospect to see that you have listened and that you have a grasp of the situation.

- Listen to what is being said. Listening well is vitally important in the sales structure

Chapter eight

Handling Objections

So what about objections? These can come at any time throughout the sales interview and you may have to field them by answering the objection briefly and then going on to ask the prospect an open question.

For example if the objection comes whilst you are still at the discussion stage and you haven't got enough answers to your situation questions, you will need to handle the objection and regain control of the interview by going back in with a situation question. This is because you don't have enough information at that stage to close the sale i.e. you don't yet know what feature and benefit will appeal to this prospect - you don't know what he or she is buying on.

Let's take an example of an objection that arises whilst you are still at the discussion stage of your sales interview before you have diagnosed the prospect's needs:

Prospect: 'But I can't afford to change suppliers at the moment.' **(Objection.)**

Salesperson: 'What do you mean exactly?' **(Open question.)**

Prospect: 'Well I have an agreement with them which ties me in for another year.' **(Prospect**

elaborates the objection - giving you more information.)

Salesperson: 'Well we may be able to help you with that but before we look at that more closely tell me, **how** much do XYZ Limited currently supply you with on a monthly basis?' **(Open situation question again.)**

The salesperson has regained control of the interview and is probing to get more information. The salesperson may be able to come up with a strong feature and benefit that may encourage the prospect to change suppliers. Or the salesperson may be able to buy the existing contract out if he/she has the authority to do so.

One of the most common failings in salespeople that I see is that the prospect will ask a question, or voice an objection, the salesperson will answer it and then sit back and wait for the prospect to ask another question or put up another objection. The salesperson loses control of the interview and ends up following the prospect. It is very difficult then to close the sale in this situation.

Objections and questions should be welcomed because they show interest. If you have carried out your discussion stage correctly and diagnosed the need or problem then when objections and questions arise see how far down the positive buying motivations you are. Let me recap for you.

Positive buying motivations

- **I am important**
- **Consider my needs**
- **Will your ideas help me?**
- **What are the details?**
- **What are the problems?**
- **I approve.**

Will your ideas help me?
By this stage you have diagnosed the needs of the prospect and you are demonstrating how the features and benefits of what you provide can help this prospect.

What are the details and what are the problems?
At these two stages you are receiving questions and objections from the prospect. See how far down the positive buying motivations you are - a step away from closing.

If I don't want to be sold to, or if the salesperson has not switched me over to the positive buying motivations, I don't ask any questions. I sit there whilst they go through their sales spiel and then I simply say, 'No thank you.'

You will probably find that the same objections come up time after time. Therefore be prepared for them. List them before the sales interview and prepare how you will answer them. If you meet a new objection and you feel you didn't handle it well then after the visit write it down and then think how you should have answered it. Ask your colleagues what they would have said and the next time it comes up you will be better prepared to answer it.

Golden rules on objection handling

When a prospect voices an objection listen carefully and patiently in order to understand what the objection is and to avoid argument.

Get your inner voice right – don't take the objection personally. Don't get all defensive. Tell yourself how far down the positive buying motivations you are and that objections show interest. The prospect has the right to make objections.

Don't leap in with your compensating benefit. Ask the prospect an open question to probe the objection. Is it a sincere objection or just a fob off? Has the prospect expressed what he/she really means? The open question can simply be along the lines of:

'What do you mean by that?'

'What makes you say that?'

'Really, why is that?'

The prospect will answer your question and will furnish you with more information or re-express the objection in a different way and usually make it clearer to you what the real objection is. This technique also buys you time to think how you will answer the objection but do make sure you are listening to the prospect and that your mind isn't racing on to give a benefit that is inappropriate.

> **Never assume you know what they mean.**
> **If you ASSUME you make an ASS of U and an ASS of ME!!!**

In my experience sales people are too ready to jump in with their benefits before finding out what the real objection is.

Answer the objection by giving your compensating benefit. Here you need to draw on your features and benefits. And if there is no compensating benefit, simply say so. Be sincere and honest. Do not 'flannel.' If there is a genuine disadvantage admit it. Then stress the advantages to the prospect to outweigh the disadvantage. Here you may have to draw on information gained earlier.

For example:

Salesperson: 'Yes, you're right, we are more expensive than your current suppliers. However you mentioned earlier that service was very important to you. By paying that extra you are guaranteed a 24 hour service which means you will be saving money by having less downtime and you will not be losing customers as a result. We can also arrange payment terms for you so that we can spread the costs over a longer period. If we could delay the first payment for you, so that you don't have to pay until the beginning of your new financial year, would this help you?'

Now let's take a more detailed look at this.

Yes, you're right, we are more expensive than your current suppliers. **Admit the disadvantage.**

However you mentioned earlier that service was very important to you. **Draw on information gained at the discussion and diagnosis stage.**

By paying that extra you are guaranteed a 24 hour service which means you will be saving money by having less downtime and you will not be losing customers as a result. **Give compensating feature and benefit.**

We can also arrange payment terms for you so that we can spread the costs over a longer period. **Strengthen by giving additional advantage or benefit.**

And if we could delay the first payment for you so that you don't have to pay until the beginning of your new financial year would this help you? **Convert the objection into a question and make it the basis of the close.**

Here I have asked the prospect if he would be interested in the proposition if a way can be found of solving his problem. If the objection is insincere then the prospect will probably raise another objection. Ignore the first objection and repeat the process on the basis of the second objection.

If the prospect keeps raising objections then you probably haven't carried out stages one, two and three adequately enough, that is:

**Approach
Discussion
Diagnosis.**

Go back in with open situation questions or ask yourself whether this person is really the decision maker.

So let's take a look at some common examples of objections and how to handle them. These are similar to those detailed in ***The Easy Step by Step Guide to Telemarketing, Cold Calling & Appointment Making*** mainly because the same objections come up again and again. You will have others special to your industry, service or product so you will need to list them before the sales visit and be prepared to answer them.

Objection: 'It's too expensive.'

Probe. Make it specific - ask, 'What do you mean by expensive?' Find out what they are really saying. Is it that they haven't got any money or that they can get it cheaper elsewhere? Or have they misunderstood you, or have a preconception of your pricing that is totally inaccurate?

Once you have found out what the real objection is then answer it with the compensating benefit.

For example:

'Yes, we are more expensive than XYZ Limited but with this model you don't have to keep paying out for replacement parts and what's more there is a lifetime guarantee so you will be saving money in the long run. If we were also to spread the payments over a longer period would that interest you?'

Objection: 'Sorry no budget.'

Probe. Ask, 'When will you be putting your budgets together?' If you know when their budgets are put together perhaps you can demonstrate how you can help them to save money or plan ahead.

Objection: 'How can your company handle a contract like this. You're much too small.'

Again probe. Ask what they mean by too small. What are they really saying? Here I think it is obvious that they are worried that your company won't be able to fulfill their requirements but there could be some other reason and we need to know if this is a sincere objection. What is meant by this remark? Once you have found out the real objection you can handle it by mentioning your compensating benefits. In this case you could also mention names of other customers that you deal with which the prospect may be able to identify with and therefore reassure him/her that you really can handle their needs.

> **Remember to probe. Ask 'Why?' Use good open questions and then give the compensating benefits.**

In summary

- Don't take objections personally; don't argue or disagree with them

- Get a good inner dialogue going and welcome objections, they show interest

- Make objections specific; ask probing, open questions

- Admit a disadvantage if there is one and go on to give a compensating benefit

- Strengthen with another feature and benefit that will appeal to the prospect

- If you make a mistake learn from it and vow to do better next time.

Chapter nine

Closing

The close should follow logically from the sales presentation without any hesitation but I know this is not always easy for some people.

Years ago, as a rookie saleswoman, I had a dread of closing. I told myself I couldn't do it, that I would never get the business. I was fine on everything else but asking for the order was a nightmare. Then I told myself that 'closing' as a word was out and all I was doing was helping the prospect to buy. I had an excellent product and I could genuinely help this company by selling it to them. The **'helping the prospect to buy'** opened up my mind and therefore doors into companies for me. It wasn't nearly so difficult after this. This helped me psychologically. It may help you.

> **One simple way of closing is by asking for the business. Often the fear of rejection prevents us. Be positive and have a confident manner.**

There are other closing techniques that may help you and I will now look at them in more detail.

Solving the prospect's problem close

We have already looked at this closing technique in the previous chapter i.e. if we could solve the prospect's problem or objection would he/she buy?

For example a brewery I worked with found the following objection and closing technique came up with some of their prospects:

Prospect: 'I'm a bit wary about using a small independent brewery like yours?' **(Objection.)**

Salesperson: 'Really why is that?' **(Probe open question.)**

Prospect: 'Will you be able to deliver the quantities I require?'

Salesperson: 'Yes, we can and we do regularly to other public houses of a similar size to yours and larger.' - **(give testimonials and relevant features and benefits.)**

Prospect: 'But you only deliver on a Thursday and Thursday is my day off.' **(Another objection.)**

Salesperson: 'So if we could arrange delivery for you at the beginning of the week would you be prepared to order through us?' **(Solving the prospect's problem close.)**

Prospect: 'Well I suppose if you could deliver on

Tuesday that would be OK.'

Salesperson with pen in hand and forms to the ready: 'Right, Tuesday it is. How many barrels would you like to order for the first delivery? Six or twelve?' **(Another close - the alternative close.)**

Prospect: 'Better make it fifteen.'

Sale completed.

The salesperson used two closing techniques as you can see. Initially he used the solving the prospect's problem close but then he added another close, he asked the prospect how many barrels he would like giving him an alternative to choose from.

Alternative Close

Giving the prospect an alternative will make it easier for him/her to make a decision.

Here are some further examples of this **alternative close.**

- 'So when would you like delivery, this week or next week?'

- 'Which colour would you prefer, the green or the blue?'

- 'How would you like to pay? By cheque or credit card?'

This is a very useful technique and one that works well in closing both in telephone selling and in face to face selling.

Fear Close

The fear close is used to put pressure on the prospect to make a decision then and there as you will see with the examples I have listed below:

- 'If you place your order now, at this exhibition, you will get a 20% discount.'

- 'This special offer only lasts until the end of the week so to take advantage of it you'd be advised to place your order now.'

- 'We've had a lot of interest in this model. If you leave your decision too long we may have sold out.' (Estate agents and car salespeople seem to like this one!)

- 'If you confirm the order now I could put it through with this month's orders which would guarantee you'd get delivery next week.' (I have had this close used on me a few times and it does work. When the salesman threw in a month's free trial he had it.)

And

- 'I really need this order to boost my sales figures, especially as we close the sales order book for the month today.'

- 'I've got a wife and five kids to feed, if I don't get this order I'll be out of a job!!!!' I will leave it up to you whether you want to use this one or not!

Assumptive Close

This is similar to the solving the prospect's problem close. What you are saying is that if you can satisfy the prospect on a point would he/she buy? For example:

Salesperson: 'Assuming then that we can get this model for you by Tuesday are you prepared to go ahead and place the order Mr. Jones?'

Prospect: 'Yes.'

Salesperson: ' Right then, I will just make a call to our depot and see if I can arrange that for you.'

Another example:

Salesperson: 'Assuming then that you are satisfied that complete confidentiality is guaranteed will you buy from us?'

If the prospect says that he is not sure then there are some other underlying objections that you have not uncovered. You need to find out what these are and resolve them. Ask an open question and probe the objection.

For example: 'What aren't you sure about Mr. Jones?' Then handle the objection as detailed in chapter eight and try closing again.

Buying signals close

As I have mentioned before buying signals can come through to you at any time by a show of interest. This can be in the form of the prospect asking you questions or even by raising objections as we have looked at. But it may be in the form of an expression like 'oh' or 'really.' Or you may read it in the prospect's body language, more about this in the next chapter.

By capitalising on these buying signals you can go on to close. However, many sales people are concentrating so hard on making their points that they can miss the buying signals. Look for them; listen for them in the conversation. When you have heard them, repeat or strengthen the benefit to the prospect and then close with one of the techniques mentioned.

Regardless of which technique is suitable for you remember what I said earlier:

> **Closing begins with the approach so take time to get this right.**

When you have closed the sale the tendency is to talk on and then oversell. **Don't. Change the**

subject, and get out.

In summary

- Be positive and have a confident manner. Don't be afraid to ask for the business

- Look and listen for buying signals and capitalise on them by strengthening your benefit and going on to ask for the business

- Objections are buying signals. Answer them and go on to close the sale

- The alternative close makes it easier for people to make a decision

- The fear close puts pressure on the prospect to make a decision or lose out in some way

- Another close involves solving the prospect's problem to help him/her buy

- Beware of the tendency to talk on and oversell

- Having won the business, change the subject and depart gracefully.

Chapter ten

Body language

Body language can be used to create an impression. So just as someone will form an impression of you through your choice and use of body language you can read what the other person is thinking and feeling through the use of their body language.

In order to be an effective salesperson therefore you need to be aware of your own body language and to be able to interpret the use of the prospect's body language. You can also use body language to build rapport with the prospect.

Some people are very good at disguising their body language; others tend to wear their heart on their sleeve. Their emotions are quite clearly visible through their expressions and how they stand or shift position.

You need to develop an awareness of how you use your body language and this is where undergoing role-play in front of a video camera can be helpful. You will quickly see whether or not you have any bad habits that need to be corrected.

You also need to understand some of the body language signals, to look for and interpret them at the same time as you are driving the sales structure through and listening to your prospect, so it is not that easy to do. In addition, something that you may interpret as a telling body language signal may just be a habit, so you will need to be able to discriminate between these.

Listed below are some body language signals you need to be aware of. But you will need to remember that different nationalities have different body language signs so if you are selling internationally or to different cultures within your own community you need to be aware of what these body language signals are.

Distance - personal body space

This can vary so you will need to know what is acceptable to people of different nationalities. Generally speaking, with British nationals, the personal space distance is about three feet hence the old saying 'Keeping them at arms length.' An arms length is three feet. When we know and like someone we allow him or her to get much closer to us. So do be careful you don't loom in at people. This is also why you shouldn't place anything on the prospect's desk without asking his/her permission; the desk is their personal space.

Body Movements

Watch for movements in the prospect's body language. For example do they lean forward when you say something, if they do that shows interest in what you have just said. If they sit back, fold their arms or rub their ear that means they don't much like what you are saying, find out why that is by asking an open question.

Rubbing the eyes can mean that the person doesn't like what they see, equally it could mean they are tired, or have something in their eye. You need to look at the other body language signals that are being sent. For example has the person shifted position, moved away from you? Or have you just shown them a brochure or catalogue or given a demonstration of a piece of equipment and perhaps they are not keen on what they are seeing?

People who put their **hand over their mouth** when speaking are often said to be lying. This may be so but it can also be a habit with some individuals. I once worked with a young woman who always did this and when I told her about it she said she had formed the habit because she had once suffered with skin problems and had been embarrassed by it and wanted to cover it up. Again, if someone covers their mouth when they are speaking to you look for any movements in body posture, any shifting of position and dropping of eye contact. If you get all three the prospect is probably not telling the whole truth.

Rubbing the neck can often mean someone is tired but it can also mean the individual is embarrassed about something. Again, do any other body language signals accompany this gesture?

You can also build rapport by **mirroring the prospect's body language** but not in an obvious way. You can move forward when they do and gently ease yourself back in the seat when they do. Don't mimic of course, just subtly mirror.

Facial Expressions

This can say it all. Frowning, looking puzzled, surprised, interested, and bored. There is no secret to reading this body language except the ability to train yourself to look for it and recognise it when you see it.

Eye Contact

Make sure you give good eye contact. If your prospect isn't looking at you, or doesn't want to look at you, try and get him or her talking. He or she will need to bring eye contact up. Once someone does you can lock onto it. If they look away you can do the same and then try and get it back again. And watch for when you do win eye contact. Does it mean that you have just said something of interest to the prospect?

I remember pitching to a group of partners in a legal firm to win them as a marketing client. There were about fifteen of them seated around a boardroom table. At that stage I didn't know who the main decision maker was. I couldn't go on the basis of it being the senior partner as he might not have been the decision maker, or key influencer, in this case.

Whilst I was giving my presentation I was receiving a few smiles and nods from a few friendly faces. The danger then is to play to these friendly souls rather than to those not looking at you. One man in particular was busy writing, sitting well away from the table and not giving me any eye contact. His body language was telling me he was superior to the proceedings and that he didn't think he needed me at all. He was very much in the first stages of the negative buying motivations.

By his superior, non-participatory body language I judged him to be the main decision maker. I needed to get and keep his attention if I was to win the contract. Half way through my presentation I started talking about the image of a legal firm being extremely important and his head came up and he gave me eye contract.

I discarded the rest of my presentation and focused solely on image. He had given me a clear buying signal through his body language. I asked a couple of questions, he started answering them and yes, I won the contact.

Body Posture

Avoid giving out defensive gestures (although you may be on the receiving end of them) i.e. closed body language. This means crossed legs, crossed arms and sitting well back and stiffly in your seat.

You will also find that hostile or defensive people will either be avoiding eye contact with you or giving you hard eye contact. If your prospect is doing this then you know you are definitely on the **negative buying motivations; i.e. I don't trust you - I don't need you**.

Get the prospect talking about himself or herself or their business and watch for the body language. When it begins to unfold and relax you know you're doing the job well and the prospect is beginning to thaw and move into the more **positive buying motivations; e.g. I am important, consider my needs.**

Maintain good eye contact with your prospect throughout the sales interview.

Sometimes you will see men shift their body language so that they **clasp their hands behind their head** thus exposing the full front of their body. This is a male body language position. Women rarely if ever sit like this and therefore do not naturally mirror this signal. This means that it puts a woman at a disadvantage and any male salesperson going into this posture will therefore not get the sale. It denotes supreme confidence which can also sometimes be read as arrogance. I would urge all salespeople not to exhibit this body language signal, either to men or women.

Impressive signals

The following is a list of impressive signals you'd do well to adopt:

- Sit upright and alert

- Sit forward to convey real interest

- Keep your eyes on the speaker

- If you need to take notes always ask if you can first. Don't take too many, as you will lose eye contact with the prospect. Jot down key points.

- Turn your body to the prospect but not head on, angle it so that it is less confrontational especially if the interview is taking place across a desk or table.

- When listening keep your body language open, no folded arms. If you have to cross your legs just cross at the ankles.

And here are some don't's

- Don't slouch

- Don't look down at notes, out of window, at the ceiling

- Don't doodle

- Don't physically turn away

- Don't fold your arms tightly across your body which says you're not listening

- Don't growl, frown, or use cynical expressions

- Don't fidget, play with your hair, tap a pen or jiggle your leg.

In summary

- Body language can be used to create an impression

- You can read what the other person is thinking and feeling through the use of their body language

- You need to be aware of your own body language and be able to interpret the use of the prospect's body language

- You can also use body language to build rapport with the prospect

- Personal distance varies from country to country

- If the prospect leans forward when you say something it shows interest in what you have just said. This is a buying signal, capitalise on it by strengthening your benefit and asking open questions of the prospect

- If the prospect sits back, folds their arms or rubs their ear that means they don't much like what you are saying

- Rubbing the eyes can mean that the person doesn't like what they see

- People who put their hand over their mouth when speaking are often said to be lying

- Rubbing the neck can often mean someone is tired but it can also mean the individual is embarrassed about something

- You can also build rapport by mirroring the

prospect's body language

- Avoid defensive gestures i.e. closed body language. This means crossed legs, crossed arms and sitting well back and stiffly in your seat

- You will find that hostile or defensive people will either be avoiding eye contact with you or giving you hard eye contact

- Maintain good eye contact with your prospect throughout the sales interview

- Sit upright and forward to convey real interest

- If you need to take notes always ask if you can first

- Don't take too many, as you will lose eye contact with the prospect.

Chapter eleven

Selling to different personalities

Finally then we return to the maxim ' People buy People.' I say finally but this is by no means the least important aspect in the selling process. It is in fact highly important. It follows that if someone likes you they are more inclined to buy from you. But everyone is different. You think you're normal but what is normal? How do you sell to people who are not like you?

To be a good salesperson you need to have an understanding of people. You need to understand that different things will motivate different people. Remember our buyer behaviour in chapter two? In addition remember our subjective reasons for buying that we examined in chapter two.

In order to provide you with a greater understanding of this I am going to look at a fairly simple model of selling to the different personality types. Obviously no-one falls into one particular 'type' and people are much more complex than I am illustrating but this will at least give you some idea of how to motivate and sell to different people.

Alongside this model you should also take into consideration a person's intellectual capacity and their behaviour, both of these will affect how they react and relate to you and likewise you to them.

As you go through the models of personality traits see if you can spot where your main personality traits lie. If you have ever undertaken a personality profile this will reveal your main characteristics both in normal circumstances and how you respond under stress. Personality traits are inherited, which is why you are often accused of being like your father or mother or a grandparent.

There are four basic 'types.' I have called them:

- **Dominant**
- **Social**
- **Measured**
- **Compliant.**

Dominant Individuals

These are people with a high degree of dominance in their personality. As a result they can be authoritative and rather superior. They are often time driven and very time conscious and therefore are intolerant of time wasters, or people they perceive as time wasters. If you hear someone say that they don't tolerate fools very easily then this is a classic Dominant statement. The superiority in their personality makes them less able to understand and relate to others who aren't like them. Dominants are usually fairly quick individuals both in speech and manner therefore if they are dealing with someone who is slower speaking or more measured in their approach, Dominants can become impatient.

Dominants can also be ambitious people so you can often find them at the top of the hierarchy but not always necessarily so. Dominants are not really team players, even if they say they are, their team is often one – themselves. They like being in control and will often take charge if in a group situation. They usually have lots of ideas and like solving problems but they do not like a lot of detail. They prefer to leave this to others.

How to recognise Dominant Individuals?

You may already have a good idea of how to recognise a Dominant. They will use dominant body language for a start. Their handshake will often be outstretched taking up more space than is normal and the grip will be very firm. In addition those with very high Dominance in their personality will often position their hand so that it is on top of yours, or they will give you the double clutch handshake, or touch the top of your arm when shaking hands. Sometimes they may hold onto your hand longer than is usual, again a very dominant statement. Their speech will be direct. They will not take time for social chitchat but will want to get right to the point. They will make flat assertions like 'You're too expensive.' Or 'Come on then sell to me' and will like putting you on the spot. They are quick decision makers and if you win one of these over you will close the sale there and then. There will be no pussy footing about and mind changing.

Selling to Dominant Individuals

Dominants are motivated by status so it is likely

they will also have the status symbols like the big car, and the big office and chair, or the expensive watch and designer accessories. They do have an ego, which again, if you recall the positive buying motivations, mentioned in chapter three, you as the salesperson will need to respond to. This prospect is saying to you 'I am even more important' so if you miss out those situation questions then you've blown it. But make sure your questions are business like, relevant and to the point.

In addition you will need to satisfy the subjective reasons for buying which could include: to satisfy and feed an ego, to satisfy the need for power and recognition.

When selling to Dominants don't give them the detail. For example don't go through the proposal step by step or they will quickly get bored and irritated and cut you short. Tell them what you're going to do for them and how you're going to save them time and make them more successful, powerful, happy etc..

Be clear, specific, brief and to the point. Use time efficiently and stick to the business in hand. You need to show that you are well prepared and that you know your product/service thoroughly. Provide them with facts and figures but don't weigh them down with them.

Social Individuals

Socials are individuals who like people and who like to be liked. Dominants don't have such a high need to be liked.

Socials are often good at selling because they are the most natural at mirroring people and at adapting a style that will suit the person opposite them. They are saying 'I want you to like me.'

Socials are adaptable, flexible and participative. These are the team players but the adaptability means they can change their minds.

Recognising a Social Individual

You may still get the firm handshake but you will not get so much dominant body language with it. The elbow will be tucked into the waist and there won't be such a firm attempt to place their hand over yours.

Status is as important to Socials as it is to Dominants so you could get the big car and the designer accessories. Where you will see the difference, and hear it, though is in the use of body language and the amount of social chitchat this person has with you. Socials will be offering you a coffee, seeing that you are comfortable, asking whether you found the office etc.. They will be putting you at your ease.

Look at the pictures on their walls. Socials will often have pictures of their families and achievements much the same as dominants will but when you ask a Social about the picture he or she will start chatting to you about the family or the golf day, whereas our Dominant individual is unlikely to talk about his or her family, will cut the social chitchat off and focus on what you've gone there for.

Selling to Social Individuals

These people are motivated by ideals and visions. So you will need to show them how your products/services can support those visions and ideals.

Leave plenty of time for socialising and relating to them and take time to socialise at the beginning of the interview. The **Approach** stage could take much longer because you may end up talking about the family or the golf swing before getting down to the business. Again, Socials are not great detail lovers so put anything technical, or all the details, in writing afterwards. Provide ideas for helping them. Pursue a supporting relationship and leave on a friendly social note. With regard to the subjective reasons for buying you are satisfying the need for respect and approval and the need to reinforce group identity.

Measured Individuals

Measured individuals are more logical and analytical. They are steady and measured in their approach. They are often security minded and don't like a lot of change. These types may be harder to sell to because they are usually sceptical and suspicious of new ideas but once you have made the sale they are often loyal.

Measured individuals are consistent and patient. They don't like taking risks and can be plodders.

However they can also be very efficient.

Many engineers fall into this category because they are attracted to that occupation by its analytical methodical approach. You can also find lawyers, accountants and professional buyers can be this personality type.

How to recognise them

Measured individuals can often be slower speaking and more quietly spoken. There will be silences in the conversation which if you have a lot of dominance in your personality can be difficult for you. You will need to curb your desire to rush in and ask another question or finish their sentences for them.

They are not motivated by status so the designer accessories and big cars etc. will be missing. In addition there will be no dominant body language. The handshake can be firm or weaker. Their dead give away though, unless they are very skilled in hiding it, is their facial expression and body language. Measured individuals will be looking at you rather sceptically. They will sit well back in their chair with their arms folded, not necessarily with hostility, but they will be holding back a judgment on you and what you are saying until they have weighed you up and they are ready to pronounce in their own mind whether they like you or not.

They will also procrastinate which makes it a lot harder for you to close the sale

Responding to measured individuals

You will need to take time to break the ice and make yourself agreeable. Your open questions are vital here. These are the people who will simply give you a one-word answer if you ask a closed question. They won't help you out like our Social individuals will.

You will need to be sincere and show a sincere interest in the prospect as a person. Take time to find areas of common ground. Be honest and open and patiently draw out the prospect's goals in a non-threatening manner. Slow down, move casually and informally. Provide lots of assurances and give clear specific solutions with maximum guarantees. Give them the detail. If you don't they will ask for it. These are also the people who will often know more about your product than you do - they've spent weeks or even months researching what boat or car to buy. You can't fob them off. When closing you will have to direct them. You will need to help them make up their mind but don't rush them. If you do you will lose the sale completely.

Compliant Individuals

Compliant individuals want to comply with the rules and regulations. This means they are usually very systematic, precise, hyper-efficient and bureaucratic. These people love detail, the more the better.

They can often be shy and self-effacing and will probably need a great deal of assurance. Because of this compliance in their nature they can often be easily agreeing which makes it difficult for the salesperson to know what they genuinely think and feel.

They are punctual and like punctuality in others. Coupled with a high intellect these people are attracted to jobs like systems analysts, researchers, scientists etc..

Recognising this type

With the compliant individual you may get lowered eye contact and fidgeting mannerisms. There will be no dominant body language, in fact the body language is much more likely to be submissive. The handshake can be perfunctory and not terribly firm. Compliant individuals can often speak quietly and can be vague.

Responding to them

Compliant individuals need a great deal of detail. They will want a full explanation giving reasons. You will need to give them plenty of time to make up their mind but gently direct them towards the close.

Be straightforward in your approach, stick to the business in hand and build credibility by listing the pro's and cons to any suggestions you make. Reassure them that there won't be any surprises. Be realistic and accurate and provide solid, tangible, practical evidence in the form of testimonials. They need time to make a decision just as our Measured individuals do.

And finally a word about men selling to women and women selling to men.

Men and women have different styles of communication. You will need to recognise this and play to it in your sales interview. Of course there are men with the female style of communication and females who have adopted the male style of communication but let's take a look at these different styles.

A woman's style of communication is generally more social than the male of the species. By this I mean that women need background information about one another. They will talk about their families, their houses, their holidays, their jobs, their bosses, their colleagues and their feelings and thoughts. Men sometimes call this gossiping but it isn't, not to a woman anyway. It is the female style of communication. Some men naturally have this style of communication too and consequently are very good at talking to and selling to women.

Generally though, the male style of communication is far more direct. Men don't need this social background information. They don't need to know about family and home circumstances. They see it as unnecessary.

The more **Social type of Individual** mentioned in the previous section will, if it is a man, want the social chitchat but this, man-to-man, will be based around four major areas; cars, football or sport, women and work.

If a female has more of the **Dominant Personality** then she will exhibit more of the male style of communication and therefore be more direct in her communication style. Quite often women who work in male dominated organisations, and who have reached management positions, have adopted this male style of communication either accidentally or by design.

The salesman

The **salesman** will need to ascertain whether or not the woman prospect he is selling to is a dominant personality. If she is then he will respond accordingly, be direct, leaving out the social chitchat. If she isn't then he would do well to take time to socialise more, get to know the woman as a person, find out more about her background circumstances, her likes and dislikes etc.. Some men are very wary of doing this, as they are afraid that it sounds as if they are 'chatting up' the woman. Those men with very strong male styles of communication find this very difficult. To them women are often a foreign species. All I can advise is that they should practice the **Open Questions.** This will help them sound more natural in the socialising process. And remember it is even more vital if selling to a measured or compliant female. It will take longer and more open questions to break the ice.

The saleswoman

If the **saleswoman** is selling to a male prospect then unless he has the female style of communication (which she won't know until he starts asking her about her family background) she needs to avoid any attempt at the social chitchat and talk business. Women need to be more direct in their communication with men. They need to stick to the business in hand. It will be pointless trying to relate to the man by talking about cars or football because even if she is the world's expert on both these subjects it is unlikely the man will respond. Football and cars are part of the male communication process and a woman talking on these matters can often be viewed, mentally, as invading his territory.

In summary

- To be a good salesperson you need to have an understanding of people

- You should take into consideration a person's personality, their intellectual capacity and their behaviour all of which will affect how they react and relate to you and likewise you to them

- There are four basic 'personality types.'

    Dominant
    Social
    Measured
    Compliant.

- Recognising them and responding to them can help drive the sales process forward

- A woman's communication style means she will generally need more background information about the person she is doing business with than a man requires

- The male style of communication is far more direct. Men don't need the background information

- Men selling to women therefore should take more time to find out about the woman as a person, whilst women selling to men should be more direct in their approach.

Checklist

Most common mistakes of salespeople

- Lack of preparation. This includes lack of product/service knowledge

- No knowledge and understanding of the features and benefits

- Misjudges the decision maker and ignores completely the other party in the sales process

- Poor grooming – sloppy and inappropriate for the target audience

- Likes to talk and usually about themselves and their products/services

- Opens up the conversation with his/her spiel and sticks to it

- Doesn't ask **open questions**

- Poor summarising skills – just carries on with his/her sales spiel

- Overuse of prospect's name – insincere

- Doesn't listen and can't answer the questions the prospect is asking

- Is patronising – misjudges the level of communication

- Ignores the objections or treats them defensively. Then starts to preach to the prospect

- Won't take no for an answer!

Checklist for the good salesperson

- Is genuine and sincere.

- Knows his/her products

- Is interested in people

- Listens and asks open questions

- Uses silences to good effect

- Treats objections sincerely and the prospect as an intelligent, interesting individual

- Helps people to buy by closing effectively

- Always leaves on a positive note.

Remember the sales structure A.D.D.I.N.

Approach
Discussion
Diagnose
Interpretation
Needs

By following this, and a few tips and techniques as detailed in this book, I hope you will **add in** your product or service to the prospect's life!

Happy Selling.

Other Easy Step by Step Guides in the series include:

The Easy Step By Step Guide to Marketing £11.99

The Easy Step By Step Guide to Telemarketing, Cold Calling & Appointment Making £9.99

The Easy Step By Step Guide to Stress & Time Management £11.99

The Easy Step by Step Guide to Developing Environmentally Sensitive Land £14.99

All the above guides are available on order from all good booksellers and direct from:

Rowmark Limited
65 Rogers Mead
Hayling Island
Hampshire
PO11 0PL
Telephone: 023 9246 0574
Fax: 023 9246 0574
E-mail: enquiries@rowmark.co.uk

Or via our web site www.rowmark. co. uk

Also available FREE Marketing Fact Sheets and Training courses.